Clare Best

*Excisions*

for Clive
with very
best wishes
August 2014
Clare

First published in 2011
by Waterloo Press (Hove)
95 Wick Hall
Furze Hill
Hove BN3 1NG

Printed in Palatino 11pt by
One Digital
54 Hollingdean Road
East Sussex BN2 4AA



A CIP record for this book is available
from the British Library

ISBN 978-1-906742-36-2

Acknowledgements

Thanks are due to the editors of the following publications in which some of these poems first appeared: *The Frogmore Papers, Kent & Sussex Poetry Society Folios* (2003-2009), *The London Magazine, Magma, MEAN 2, The New Writer, Poetry News, The Rialto, Smiths Knoll, The Warwick Review, Canadian Woman Studies/les cahiers de la femme*. Also *Buzz* (Templar Poetry, 2008), *The Sandhopper Lover* (Cinnamon Press, 2009), *Of Love and Hope*, ed. Deborah Gaye (Avalanche Books, 2010), *Poetry South East* 2010 (Frogmore Press, 2010), and *Did I Tell You? 131 Poems for Children in Need*, ed. Nicky Gould & Vicky Wilson (Categorical Books, 2010)

I would like to thank Peter Abbs, Patience Agbabi, Liz Bahs, Ros Barber, Niall Christie, Judith Kazantzis, Mimi Khalvati, Andie Lewenstein, Beth Miller, Jess Moriarty, Alice Owens, Jeremy Page, Catherine Smith, Monica Suswin, Fay Young, and others, for fellowship and criticism over the years. My thanks also to Christine Baker, Patrick Bond, Gabrielle Fox, Vanessa Gebbie, Zenith Gross, Heather Holden-Brown, Matthew Hollis, Celia Hunt, Kim Lasky, Celia Randell, Sarah Salway, Myra Schneider, Laura Stevens, Irving Weinman, James and Shana Wilby, and the late Ted Walker, for encouragement at key moments.

I am indebted to Helena Nelson, Catherine Smith, Janet Sutherland, Susan Wicks and Jackie Wills for close reading and generous responses. I am very grateful for a grant from Arts Council England in 2011, which helped to propel this collection towards publication. I would like to express my enormous gratitude to John O'Donoghue, the most insightful, tenacious and unflinching editor I could have wished for. And thanks to all at Waterloo Press for their dedication in producing this book.

Additional and particular thanks are due, relating to *Self-portrait without Breasts*. Thank you to medical staff at Guy's Hospital and the London Bridge Hospital, especially to Mr Nicolas Beechey-Newman. I am deeply grateful to Dr James Mackay. My thanks to Margarita Hanlon. Thank you Liz, your company and support were exceptional gifts.

Philip and Freddie, I can never thank you enough. You have been with me all the way.

By the same author

*Treasure Ground* (Happen*Stance*, 2009)

Contents

*Airborne*

# Matryoshka

*for my grandparents and my parents*

## August

I cut salvia, wild sweet peas,
the last jasmine, fuchsia
to remind him of Cornish walks,

and a fierce pink rose. I want him
to admire the vase
doubled in the mirror.

*You should have seen my garden in June—*
*all passion, colour.*
He says, *I will next year.*

Monday, the sun half down,
I tidy the room, notice
rose and jasmine gone.

He's taken them
and with them all he knows
of my high summer.

## Knowing the prognosis

After the third pink gin,
a glow like the aura of Christ

fills his kitchen, his house.
He lunches alone at the table,

shrimps downed with Sauternes,
but everything hammers and aches.

Aspirin, codeine, valium, so beautiful
these white stepping stones,

the places they take him
slow and easy with whisky and soda.

Straying from room to room,
he relives parties, the memories

thickening now, with morphine.
Here's Venus stretched out nude

on the sofa, smooth as a sister,
a daughter. How he wants her,

how he needs to hear her voice
like rain on water.

## My father's thesaurus

You've scored your name in black ink
on the cover. But the spine's
uncracked. No corners creased,
no bus tickets or receipts

signposting thoughts you tracked.
Holding the book softly
as I might a sick bird,
I stroke its fore-edge with my thumb,

coax dark openings
where you must have looked:
*Latency, Guilt, Endearment, Distortion.*
And what did you desire

from 'Abstract Relations'—
*Identity, Union, Bond?*
Without you here to lip-read
the entries, I might never understand.

## Six rendezvous with a dead man

(i) The door from the foyer swings. A slice of brightness grows and shrinks, delivering them one by one to find their seats. The band's warming up, auditorium thick with sax, bass, keyboard, drums. I'm sinking into rhythm when I catch your rich sweet scent—that cologne you've always slapped around your neck and chin each morning and again each night. The knowledge trapped within my cells, all I can keep, alone in the dark.

(ii) You sit in the ladderback chair, beside me. *Not carcinoma,* you snap, *that was the secondary cause, the primary cause was pneumonia.* The Registrar staples papers, signs fifteen copies of the death certificate. Seals them in an envelope. She clears her throat, thanks me for the cheque, asks if there's anything else before I go. You dart me that sideways look, *Let's get the hell out of here. I need a drink.*

(iii) An hour to check two hundred service sheets. You at my elbow, in your best dark suit, striking my knuckles with your metal rule each time the print is anything but monochrome. Copy by copy I discover magenta raked across lines of type, yellow and blue smearing the space between the second hymn and the Committal. Some copies are clean. You tell me to pile those neatly in a box marked *GOOD.*

(iv) I find the Bitter Aloes when I'm clearing shelves. The cap sheds crystals as I twist and pour the tincture onto my palm. Dip in the tip of my tongue. I'm six again, you're painting all my fingers and both thumbs. Later, in bed, I suck and suck until the gall inhabits my mouth. The juices do their work, purge my sins, seal my lips. Time goes on. You add bitters to your nightly gin. I understand that I need punishing.

(v) The swimming hour: down and back. All the years: down and back. No need to think of you, no need to look. Down and back: learning to forget. Perhaps you never lived. Stretch, kick, breathe; under, up and breathe. Down and back. Vision alternating between silent fluid world and air above. Then I see you. At the deep end, by the clock, your right index finger beckoning. That way you have.

(vi) I wait in the cold for the people who take away stairlifts and deathbeds, the paraphernalia of a long decline. Standing in room after room, I seek your absence, as if the print of you here is the proof I want. You're gone. Not for me the desire to touch your clothing or pull the hair from your comb. And when the bedroom door closes on its own, I welcome your invisibility, the mystery that's parted your matter from mine.

## The death of Perses

> Perses had a daughter, Hecate,
> who surpassed her father in boldness and lawlessness...
> And since she possessed great experience in such matters
> she poisoned her father.
> *Diodorus Siculus, Library of History*

Bluebottles crawl his bed in search of meat—
each lacquered fly the size of passion-fruit.
He tells Hecate these things.

Out in the black, the moon leans on its rump
by a stand of yews, their twisted bodies layered
through centuries on chalk.

Hecate dreams. She leads him there, props him
in the toxic shade, cuts sapwood for a cot,
gathers a feast of deathberries.

One by one, she packs the soft jewels
in his mouth. *You're delivered.*
*Here's water and a torch to pierce the night.*

*

No path among the yews, no way
to tell which rusty limbs are branch or root—
        all incest growth. It's dark, no looking back
and the ground littered with flint.

At last she's out, wind cool on her face.
She makes for the hill, some distance
to recall his words, *I loved you*
        *the way I knew.*

She watches farina billow like smoke
from the forest floor, tease
and drift above the canopy of ancient crowns—
dew and pollen fused in a deadly gas
        and the sun rising.

## Uncoupled

Dual carriageway. The driver accelerates. I shift
on the leather seat. The comb holding my veil
pulls at my scalp. My father
looks at his watch.

At the level crossing the barrier's down.
Pews must be filling. We wait.
*I checked,* he says, *there shouldn't be one now.*
Knuckles white in his lap.

The organ's playing Sheep May Safely Graze.
I should be there. But we're stuck.
Road works, men in hard hats,
the one-way system blocked.

A hundred yards to go. *Shall I walk?*
He won't hear of it, won't hear of his daughter
arriving on foot for her wedding.
*You will be driven.*

We arrive. The driver opens the door.
Silk everywhere, my father
everywhere. Flowers, veil. Up the steps.
Loose pointing in the red brick porch.

No looking back, no
looking back. Here we are
for the last time,
arm in arm.

## Taking my father

The last of yesterday's snow
drips through a privet hedge
across the street. You're here,
in the passenger seat—and
we're fifteen minutes early.
You complain about dog hair,
sweet wrappers, blunt pencils,
the tax disc nearly expired.
Twice you check your watch.
I ask if you want to come in
this time. Your silence says *No.*
So I leave you to tidy the car,
knowing your eye will be on me
as I walk. Knowing, if you came
you'd just sit rigid in the chair,
the tissues on the table
well beyond reach.

## Family walk

They follow him down her favourite path,
his right hand smoothing cobweb hair, his left
swinging the blue-striped Tesco bag.
His golf shoes bruise the leaves, he talks
of a holiday in the Algarve.

At last, the end of the hollow way—
the field beyond seems the right place,
where woods peel back to sky,
where salt and gulls blow in from the sea.

*By the fence*, he says. They stand.
He takes from the bag
five white polystyrene picnic pots.
*We'll each scatter some of her*
*here*, he says. *That's fair.*

## Afterwards

I drive you home on black roads through winter hills,
you thank me for the silence,
for taking it steady;

I fetch lilies and roses in from the car,
we sit on facing sofas
drinking coffee the colour of mud, wordless

until I offer to put flowers in water.
Then you take me to the dresser crowded with jugs
and show me

her flower scissors in their leather sleeve,
drawers full of plastic packets—
Cut Flower Food.

She saved them up over the years,
no more than half a sachet for a bunch, and now
there are all these.

## Orpheus

Turning
he sees her cheek like a peach
her damson lip

knows for a moment
ripeness
the promise of touch

before dust fills his mouth
before
the undoing—

everything
split
from itself.

## Taboo

(i) *I am collected from school*
He opens the passenger door for me, slams it shut. His face reddens, greys again. He walks round the back, checks the boot, sinks into the driver's seat. At last he speaks. *Your mother couldn't come for you today ... hospital ... an operation. Nothing serious.* He twists the key in the ignition. And all the way home he drives in the middle of the road saying, *Don't worry, everything will be all right. Everything will be all right.*

(ii) *I am taken to the hospital*
The end of the lino, a barred window high in the gloss wall ahead. Door to the left. *Stay here,* he says, *I'll fetch you.* Night blacks out the panes. I wait and wait. The door is finally opened, onto white. He has pulled the sheet to her neck, smoothed the pillows, bathed her eyes and cheeks. The words have been stuffed back in her mouth. She has set her lips in a smile. Her right hand crawls from the bedclothes, reaches out.

(iii) *I prepare for my mother's return*
He asks me to draw curtains across windows, turn up radiators. *Your mother will be cold.* He selects three dresses from the wardrobe, lays them out on the bed, tells me to choose one for my mother to wear home. *The blue,* he suggests. When he has packed the case and driven away, I drag light into corners, stack it under the stairs. I unlock the garden door and let birdsong inside the house.

(iv) *I listen to the unpacking*
She comes in, stopping to stroke the dog. He brings the case upstairs sets it down on the rack, offers to help. From the hall I hear metal catches snap back, zips unzip, bottles clank onto the dressing-table top, the clunk of close-fitting drawers. I whisper through the keyhole, *I'm here when you need me,* and sit on the floor, counting the days on the amber beads of my bracelet, guarding the bedroom door.

(v) *I am left in charge*
I am hungry, lonely. No-one calls. Just the clock ticking in a house of dust and ghosts. I go down to the kitchen, pile a tray with Rich Tea biscuits, packets of raisins. Jug of rusty water. Bowl of light. Climb upstairs, knock. He sits unmoving in the velvet chair, eyes staring forward. In the bed, my mother, facing the window, asleep. Next to my mother, myself. I place the tray at the foot of the bed, tiptoe away.

## Stopping distance

*i.m. HEB*

The surgeon told her not to drive
until she could make a full emergency stop;
hill starts were bad enough—

two tons hung on one butchered arm
but she was never ready
for the screech of tyres—and so she kept

her distance from the car in front,
hoping she wouldn't need
to close that gap. Like this

she drove for years without a belt—
foot on the accelerator,
*Tristan und Isolde* cranked right up.

## Feast

It is no surprise when the old walls crowd us
around the family table, how we

lean together in December sun, dizzy
from our early waking. Each time

we are ready for her slipping away,
his drawing the curtains, turning out the lights,

and when she returns, miraculous
green-blue flames play over the dish—

the same as last year and next, until
we blink and suddenly the blaze is gone.

No surprise as she passes plates,
three, four, five, the familiar

mouth after mouthful
of sweet dark mass,

our slow urgent search
for edge or surface, the sixpence

bright as a bit between teeth,
heavy and blunt on the tongue.

# Stitch

My grandmother knew about seams, knew
things made from good material
may be cut and made again.

When a sheet wore thin in the middle
my mother and I laid it across the floor,
folded it once, lengthwise,

corner to corner. As we pulled it taut
my grandmother split it with shears.
We turned each half

sides to middle. On hands and knees
she pinned, then tacked them together
with Sylko, *Bottle Green.*

She worked the treadle, humming
the Skye Boat Song. We passed the linen
into her hands, making the old sheet new.

My grandmother knew about seams—
her abdomen ruched from pubis to sternum,
the stitch-marks silver and blue.

## Finding my aunt

Light from the passage falls
	on the fancy sheet, giant bed.
Light in a triangle
	cornering her and her baby.

She's bare to the waist,
	each blue-veined breast
bigger than his head.
	*Stay with us*, she says.

Lost in her flesh
	he snorts like an animal.
My breath's caught,
	can't let it go again.

## Play

The boys hop like peg-leg pirates,
we chase them, trip them up.
When they stretch their mouths
to letterboxes, we flare our nostrils,
shriek until they bolt.

Once they're out of sight
we kneel in the bushes, lift our shirts,
poke belly-buttons, fold nipples
so they disappear.

My mother whispers in my head:
*Be careful. If the wind changes*
*you'll stay like that.*

## Blaze

Is it like this?

My brothers' domain. *In*, where I shouldn't go—Spitfires and Messerschmitts hang on threads in the darkening air.

Isn't it just like this? The quiet afternoon. Trestle table drawing-pinned with paper, littered with Airfix paints. Camouflage Grey, Khaki Drab. Pots of sable-hair brushes. Tubes of glue. A half-built Russian tank. Dead bluebottles; daddy longlegs everywhere.

Hard to strike a match against the little strip. I try and try. At last it flashes into life, sears my thumb. Drop it—smoulder smoke. Then flaring print, flames scorching the Russian tank. A bottle of water––quick quick—unscrew the cap—pour—but *Oh! Oh! Oh!* the liquid fuels the fire, makes it gasp and leap to the boarded ceiling in a rush of light and heat.

Beyond fear now. Part of me stays to watch the fire take—red, orange, yellow in a fiery fountain—whoosh—frizzle—spit. Part of me runs—down, along the passage, down more stairs to the kitchen, yelling *Fire! Fire!* Out of breath.

And isn't it like this?

She turns from the sink, and she's past me, shouting *Don't move*! Up, up, an angel to the top of the house (I didn't know she could fly).

Later she tells me she put the fire out with the big red extinguisher and her prayers. *And Never*, she says, *Never Never Never Never Again.*

Now I light matches in my head. Let them drop. I choose when to tip white spirit on the blaze. I stand at the centre—fire circling, wrapping, keeping me safe.

It is like this.

## Bath

I am four years old.
My bath is the kitchen sink
on a January night. An engine wind.

The air's crumpet warm, familiar.
On the stove a massive pan
hisses steam from its chimney lid.

My mother's voice, close, humming
as she lifts me, sits me on scrubbed wood.
She hugs me in a rough towel, rubs my back.

I look beyond her,
over the cliff of her shoulder—
a green sea crashing in.

# Circus, Santa Catarina

A few arcs of seats. A peroxide signora taking coins for candyfloss. Up front: a school desk, a chair propped on Barolo bottles, and Luigi—long grey hair, striped vest, elastic-waisted pants. At his side his youngest, with her red curls, her jewel-encrusted ears. She sets up act after act. Climbs the walls like an insect. Now she's through the hoop—wrists elbows knees hips, balancing a carafe of water on her head.

When she flattens onto splintered wood, he traces her silhouette in blades. He has her measure. *Please papa, no fire tonight.* But he whispers, *I must have fire on New Year's Eve.* And he lights a fist of torches one by one. She sees beyond this room to mountains, a black sky pricked with stars. The old year's frost-bitten, dying, and he swallows fire, bringing flame after flame to darkness in his throat.

## matryoshka

this is great-grandmother
holding the past the future
life within life
years of dancing, burying the dead
she sits and sits not wanting sleep
eyes wide open

this is grandmother
holding the baby who cries and grows
the weight of the child
keeps her feet on the ground
they have the same hands
she and the child

this is mother
her green eyes full of the sea
she brings fish and bread to the table
and feeds them all, they eat and eat
she cannot rest
she's tired tired

this is the girl ready to bud
the girl with the blue bird
dreaming a boy, his laugh, his kiss
the weight of his hips
she holds the bird to her breast
and sleeps

this is the baby held and held
and held and held
this is the baby
holding the apple she can't yet bite
this is the weight
the grievous weight

this is great-grandmother
grandmother
tired mother loving the child
the girl with the blue bird
the baby
the seed

## The final week

This time, I will be in charge. Without warning
I will trap cattle, reptiles and all other animals (clean

and unclean) along with every child, woman, man;
as the last rains fall, rivers shall swell and bleed,

spending themselves and congealing into mud;
I will forbid the rainbow, fill the sky with toxic gas,

grass and trees shall wither, fruit shall spoil on the vine;
birds shall spin to the ground, mid-flight,

dolphin and whale shall be tossed like flotsam
on crimson seas; there will be no telling day from night,

right from wrong. When I command the hurricanes,
the deep shall rise and devour the land;

and once I have extinguished stars and sun and moon,
the darkness and the abyss will be mine.

## Who

I am the page ripped from the book
missing and unknown

I am a key without a lock
a peach inside a stone

I am the child running the track
and the sharp right turn

I am quick to learn how not to speak
I am flame that will not burn

# Self-portrait without Breasts

*for Pippa*
*and for all the others*

## Self-examination

Get to know your breasts. Near the armpit
you may find pebbles, bladderwrack, pearls.
This is normal. Don't be alarmed.

The lower part of your breast
could be gravel. There might be silt,
quicksand, shifting dunes under the nipple.

Check for flotsam at low tide. Search
for a rock in shingle, a limpet on the sandy beach.
Seek help if you discover these.

## Vital statistics

### (i) The consultant puts it like this

*Most breast cancers are sporadic.*
*Only five percent*
*genetic—a defective gene gives the woman*
*an inherited predisposition. So when*

*two or more close relatives*
*develop the disease, we must*
*be vigilant. If one parent has a bad gene*
*there's a fifty-fifty chance you have it.*

*If you do (we can test*
*for two genes—there are others*
*not yet found) the risk of cancer's*
*eighty-five percent. How does that sound?*

### (ii) Eighty-five percent

Eighty-five percent of computers in China are infected with viruses
Eighty-five percent of lost umbrellas are left on long-distance buses
Eighty-five percent of embryos transferred during IVF fail to be born
Eighty-five percent of men over sixty spend Sunday mowing the lawn
Eighty-five percent of sunscreens don't deliver their marketing claims
Eighty-five percent of people want children in another part of the plane
Eighty-five percent of western women wear the wrong bra size
Eighty-five percent of English tomorrows have weather just like today's

## The surgeon's album

He turns the pages for me:
full and partial reconstruction, implants,
muscle flaps from back and stomach. Creations
to match and balance. *But how would I look*
*flat? No extras. Straightforward scars.*
He frowns at a lop-sided photo.
*The absence doubled? I've not done that before.*

Twelve months on, he wants
my picture, conforming to house style:
no head, arms at forty-five degrees to clavicle.
I stand anonymous against a stripped pine door,
knots and fissures dark behind my skin—
a knife-thrower's object, still
until the last blade hangs from the wood.

## Two weeks before surgery

*Cast me and I will become what I must be*

We've oiled my shoulders, collarbone,
breasts—olive-scented, shiny
as greased rubberwood, I'm primed for casting.
You soak chalky bandages, wrap me

in slapstick layers of white—
a sacrament to tender body and life.
Working fast before the plaster sets
we smooth wet dressings onto slippery skin—

keep my contours, take my shape;
at every fold and ruck we stop, look closer
to remember. I lie death-still, encased,
breath slow-drawn, not to crack my shell:

an end and a beginning. Beneath the carapace
I hum a lullaby—you lift the curves away,
cast off my breastplate,
air moving like shadow over sentenced flesh.

## Countdown

Three turns in the corridor
to the anaesthetic room, one last walk
with breasts, the weight of them
familiar as my own name and address.

A young man in a white coat small-talks
London, fixes a cannula into the wrist
where my watch has been. My lips
keep moving—explain we left
some years ago, not the stress,
more the desire to raise our child
on chalk hills, near the sea.

His eyes clear as a newborn's
close to my face, he holds my hand—
a moment of love, I will call it that.
I lend him this life, veins freezing
from the forearm up.

Technical steps

Patient supine, arms right-angled to torso,
breasts and axillas exposed
(no Paralyzing Agent to be used in anaesthetic)

*the embryo's mammary ridge,*
*a thickened strip of ectoderm*
*at six weeks' gestation, develops and extends*

Prepare chest with antiseptic. Check:
Clamps, Vascular Hemoclips,
Blake Drains, Skin Stapler, Marking Pen

*a segment of this ridge*
*persists in the thoracic area and proliferates,*
*budding multiple lactiferous ducts*

Draw island to include Nipple-Areola,
make incision, retract skin flaps,
dissect breast from Pectoralis Major muscle

*a small pit in the epidermis*
*ultimately becomes*
*the nipple*

## Recovery room

Before you surface, they select
a pair of eyes from a tall jar by the door.
Checking for colour, they push them into place.

The shade they paint your face, *Warm White,*
matches the walls, it will stay bright
for days. Next they give you a nose

that detects only latex, aftershave,
surgical scrub. The younger nurse
attaches ears, tunes them in, adjusting

the volume while she speaks a name;
it sounds alien, metallic, definitely not yours.
Teeth and tongue are slipped in quick

so you can articulate: *Is it tomorrow?*
*My lips are dry. How do I know if I'm dead?*
Blood pressure's stable now, a top-up

of analgesic and you're set for the ward.
But first they smuggle into your skull
random clips from someone else's memory—

you'll discover them later, at the edge of sleep.
As they wheel you out, you request
a glass of water, some extra air.

## I think of love

and suddenly as though I've heard some new word
in a half-known tongue, comes
this sense of you, and in the opiate fog a growth of light
and you there just beyond my reach

to make me stretch, fill my lungs
and feel the cuts,
a tightening band of steel around my ribs—
and all the years and days we've been together count

as much as every stitch that binds me skin to skin,
and in the places nipples were
I feel a charge of blood
and ghosts of kisses visit me as pain.

# Prey

River boats carve up and down,
commuters trail to work in lines
over London Bridge.

An eagle has bedded its claws
in my chest. I hang by the city wall,
watching, waiting to heal.

## Breast care nurse

She whistles in—flat shoes, primary colours,
wide smile:

*Remember to take some softies when you leave—*
*use them as soon as your wounds are closed,*
*wear them with a comfy bra, baggy top,*
*nobody'll guess. Then call and make a date*
*for silicone ones, any size you fancy, they'll look good*
*under a T-shirt or vest. Try different brands*
*till you find what suits—so many kinds,*
*even stick-ons for nights.*

I want to tell her
I am my own woman-warrior,
heart just under the surface. I let go of pretence
weeks before the surgeon drew
his blue arrows on my chest.

## Following the others

This body's bruised and torn
with frostbitten openings
where black winds howl.

Others crossed this frozen waste,
edging forward, finding their way
as I find mine now.

## The new geometry

I'm laid out, my head padded
in the angle of the back seat,

the belt above ruling its hypotenuse
across my space, placing me

in the sudden angularity of the world.
This line of sight's ideal

to study the oval heads of cyclists,
oblong posters pasted on oblong buses,

faces squared in fogged-up windows.
Now we accelerate, switch lanes,

I see plane trees in parallel rows,
parabolas of lights. A trapezium of sky.

Over the South Circular, a helicopter
poised like a rotating star.

## Removing sutures in the bath

Lap of water, deep
water, stitched
and rippled skin. Look

through fluid glass
to winter sky—
jet trails,

each quick cut
straight and white—
slow, the vapour

spreads, deforms,
reshapes. Impossible
to think

tomorrow's
clear
and blue.

## Self-portrait without breasts

Tangled hair, charcoal-socket eyes,
mouth slack after one more long night
restless on my back. This body's fenscape,
manscaped, hills removed—the meaty joins
still livid, tight shut mouths
where distant territories were stitched

in touch. Blood seeps in deltas over ribs,
yellow and purple track to the waist.
*You're even more beautiful now,* you say
and I believe, for though I never was, I am
explorer, seeker—I've travelled
and I have an ear for truth.

## Memento

When you cast me, I held my breath
as the plaster set. You kept your focus,
capturing the contours of my breasts.

Remember that awkward fold by the clavicle,
air trapped between layers, remember
my fear—that flesh could not be cast

to look like flesh. But now, when I touch
the rough white woven skin, I want to quit
my body, let the twin chalk rind

contain my breath, while I recall a lover's kiss,
the heat of milk-tight flesh, my newborn
trying to focus as I held him.

How will I remember this?
Numb flesh stapled over ribs,
my breath snagged within.

## The nipple place

I mourn this most of all—
the grief acute and physical.
Sensation prickles in the numb
scar, tells me of the place
my left breast was, a phantom
where the nipple lies in space
somewhere in front of me,
gathering nerve and duct,
concentrating me
in skin—excite, contract.
A meeting place, the place I met
those few, those so few loves
that time would prove
could turn me inside out.

## Flat lands

Expanse of skin stretched over ribs:
this is the new terrain we'll trace on paper—

a detailed plan with code and key.
Our way to measure and record

how much feeling has been lost, how much
might be retrieved.

Let's cross-hatch regions of polar snow—
uninhabited, no sensation.

In places, the surface won't tell the truth:
mud on top of frozen soil and rock.

We map this permafrost with stars
held in parentheses.

Some areas are fragile: thin ice
on a lake—a leaf or feather settling

could start the crack, the thaw. We know
to plot these zones with question marks.

## black and white

if it's light when I wake
and if I look left I see
this three-month me

wrists against chest
fingers tip to tip
palms floating over ribs

she stares from the frame
sternum lifting and sinking
hands filling with breath

## Clear-out

seamless sports tops, sweated, grey as gum
lilac camiknickers, Paris '92, unworn

shocking pink bustier (supplementary pads)
disposable paper pants for handbags

*Jockeys for Her*, folded, half-priced
camisoles—laced, flowered, satinised

coloured thongs curled like exotic snakes
precious silks in cream and caviar black

bra-and-pantie sets from magazines
sequinned, crotchless, stuff of dreams

long-desired C cups with double Lycra straps
zips, poppers, neat breast-feeding flaps

underwired wonderbras to lift morale
empty drawer—no underwear at all

## Amazons

We are warriors, women marked by a lack of breast—
bows crafted from elm, sinew and bone,
axes double-edged.

We live on our wits, we live on the move.
Tomorrow at dawn we ride—
our arrows will find their kill. But tonight

we hush our restless mares,
lie together on leopard skin, kiss each other's scars,
stare into the fire where shadows dance.

## Representation

The window-dresser strips
nine skinny girls, slow-dancing each.
Look, it's the turn of the tall brunette—

pert breasts, absurdly elongated legs,
good for tango and two-step,
then she's propped with the rest.

In the morning, the dresser will wrestle
her troupe into this season's layers,
help them strike the right pose. But now

she flips the *Closed* sign, sets out for home.
I slip in at the back, lower the blind,
twist off the brunette's top half.

The torso I give her is Topman—
discrete pecs and six-pack.
Shoulders just broad enough.

## No adhesive necessary

Past the Hide 'n Seek lingerie range, beyond Naughty Nurse and Hail Mary sets, to a screened-off area with rows of jelly-coloured vibrators and Jiggle Balls. By the time I'm examining a five-foot inflatable penis, she's close. *Need any help?* That confidential smile. *Yes, do you have nipples?* She's not sure, she'll check. *I've lost mine,* I add.

At home, I press the salmon-coloured discs back to back—a miniature UFO—then peel them apart, lick their flat sides, choosing where to place my one-size nipples: near or far, high or low. They sit over the stripes of white scar like elastoplast. Under a T-shirt they appear home-grown. When I touch them they're always firm.

## Projection

I reach up, pull it down. The shadow
thrown against the screen
is the same that patterned the wall

but since the backdrop's white
and clean, my stare persistent,
long, I see at last a me I've never seen.

## Last

Who can say when the last time was—
last time you kissed my breast?
I don't recall
it seems like years ago.

All last times move together
and I wonder
is this how last is—

was the last time you kissed me
the last poem I read, the last time we spoke
the last pebble I collected from the beach
the same day the last snow fell?

Is there a crowded place
where all last things are—
all letting go?

# Intercession

*Thoughts on a painting of Saint Agatha*
*by Francisco de Zurbaran*

Virgin martyr, protector
of valleys, wet nurses, bell founders—
invoked against breast disease,
earthquakes, eruptions of Mount Etna.
Agatha, whose breasts were excised

with pincers by order of a jilted lover,
what do you make of these reconstructed
bodies? Muscle flaps. Tissue expanded
by balloon. Thigh and buttock flesh
ingeniously transposed. Do you admire

the silicone implants, the polished skin—
nipples grafted from earlobes and labia,
areolas tattooed? You stand there
serene, flat-chested, forever the girl,
bearing your breasts on a dish

and if people mistake the hemispheres
for handbells or perfect loaves of bread,
help them remember—each of us
has severed parts
we carry separately.

## Consolations

Our hearts are closer
when we hug, no bra to grey

and ruin in the wash, less
bounce and wobble

running for a bus,
full horizontal contact

with the ground, I am
streamlined

in air and water, I remind myself
of me—and you

press your ear to this ribcage,
hear me live.

## Gaze

You want a publicity shot
so I send a black-and-white (pre-op, nude,
cropped—I am sure—to shoulders and head).

But when you double-click
I'm all there, as I was. You have me
full-breasted, goose-fleshed in that attic studio.

If we meet, will your gaze
be lingering, forensic? Will you recall
light striping my cleavage like evening sun on dunes?

Will your eye undress, redress me,
trying to reconcile that image
with the shape I've shifted to?

# Seduction

When they lie together now
they make new kinds of love. Her fingers

trace the gash above his brow
that bled against the cellar step last year;

her breath cools a ring of purple skin
around a grainy scar. There are

the usual homely marks—tip of iron
to thumb, oven's edge to wrist, taut patch

from scalding milk the day their boy
turned six. Such tenderness for each

and for the cicatrice where she was torn
and stitched that night the baby came;

the nine-inch stripes of platinum
across her chest, where breasts have been

excised, remembered, grieved
and almost, now, forgotten.

## Account

*In 1811 the writer Fanny Burney underwent a mastectomy,*
*without anaesthetic, at her home near Paris.*
*She later recorded the experience in her journal.*

Four carriages stop in the street.
One last mouthful of wine
before I ascend the bed,
two nurses at my side.

Three chimes of the clock.
Seven men in black, seven
full glasses of claret.
Nine stacks of compresses, lint.

A cambric veil across my face,
the glitter of burnished steel
and backlit by sun,
a forearm over my chest.

The surgeon's index finger
describes a line, a circle, a cross.
Six incisions and he changes hands.
My screams, throughout.

## All this

All this will go on changing,
you'll recover some feeling
and the scars
will flatten and fade.

*When will the first crocus show;*
*which day will the bud split its calyx?*
*Will damselflies hover like summer coming*
*and before summer will there be spring?*

There are signs already—
roots stirring
and that chrysalis at your shoulder
unfolding spangled wings.

## The bookbinder

Pare the leather, thin the skin
where it must stretch and crease.
Then paste: the tanned flesh darkens,

wet and chill, fingers working
over spine and cords, into joints,
mitreing corners neat and flat.

Bandage the book in paper, let it
settle under weights, day after day
until the leather's dry and tight.

When the time is right for finishing,
black the room, clamp the book
spine up in the beech-wood press,

the lamp pointing where to begin.
Hot brass letters and a vigilant hand—
an accurate blind impression.

Paint in glair with a fine brush,
lay on gold leaf, with level breath.
Tilt the light, shadows will reveal

the place to press the tool again.
Now, strike the gold—feel the title
word by word, bright in the grain.

Airborne

*to those few, with love*

## Airborne

Summer folds over Sussex a July afternoon
when the earth's curve is enough to make me gasp,
let alone this being in the air with you.

We fly spires and downland, dip and sputter
above my mother's garden. She's heard us coming,
she's on the lawn jumping and waving.

We circle three times. She's still waving as you loop
the loop, scramble my world a second time.
She's there weightless, cheering, upside down.

I'm trapped in the helmet, near delirious,
rapid with fumes and altitude
and being alone, with you.

## Lost

The morning's summer-skinned,
not a morning for a funeral.
There's no escaping
the lightness of the box
covered with layers
of pleated white paper,
more like a writing box,
a case for a rare trophy.
It is not a twelve-inch coffin.

She places on the white box
a neat twist of lavender,
deep red rosebuds,
sage and rosemary
from her garden.
They put the box
on the back seat of the car
and she sits next to it, resting
one hand on the unfixed lid.

At the crematorium,
there's too much time.
The papers are all
in order. The chapel's
dusk dark, heavy,
and here the box looks
even lighter and too small
lying on the catafalque,
so white and on its own.

## Another advent

The innkeeper sleeps, hearing no late knock.
Mary and Joseph continue their journey
childless, to be taxed.

Shepherds endlessly watch
their stony flocks.
Angels never come.

Stars fail to shine, wise men
go wandering aimlessly on. Holly and ivy
hang uncut in woods. Carols are not sung.

## second son

if I'd known then
how this would be

the infinite
keen lack of you

the sting still vivid in me
where you grew

if I'd known the sentence
days becoming years

if I'd foreseen your fingers
uncurling in my hand

if I'd imagined you'd always be with me
what then?

## lullaby without voices

he's with them still
    the one who wasn't born
with them in the night

waking to a bright half-moon
    sky and clouds
all shades of blue and grey

they're sure he's with them
    still the little one
who had no time

shifting   dark
    between them
a phantom in their boat

## Unknown place

Fen winds leaned at doors,
black pressed against the window glass—
we were nine hours under in that linen bed

in that house we didn't know. Sometime
between sundown and cockcrow
I surfaced, breathing quick salt breaths,

dark unwrapping me, my need for you
reaching where you should be.
I found you beached, beyond words,

skin hot as August flagstones.
I lashed your arms around me,
took you in.

## Honeymoon, Galicia

A donkey brays in the fog,
taking turns with foghorn and lighthouse
to keep us awake.

We split wood for the stove,
fill a cauldron with opal onions, garlic curses,
pink flint potatoes, skin-burst tomatoes,
dark fingers of wine-soaked bacon,
stock of a chicken raised on salt and maize.

We light a fire, breathe steam and smoke,
hear the soup tumble, the pan
shudder its lid.

## Partners

He dreads *insides*:
seed caves in peppers,
peas loaded snug in the pod,

sliced apples that sweat
before turning brown, intricate
cabbage maps.

Bisected melons
make his hands shake; he steers clear
of salad—lettuces provoke

a certain frisson, layer after layer
of insides—too imaginable, too
near unwrapped.

Her fear is the *outside*
masking detail underneath.
She can't look

when he handles dimpled oranges,
slick aubergines,
hirsute kiwi fruit.

His gift to her: a beef tomato,
metal-scented, warm from the vine.
He shuts his eyes—

she opens hers, takes the red fruit,
raises the knife. One stroke
slices through,

drawing raw beauty—
patterned secrets
outed, split.

## Tail lights

Driving behind you in fog, not quite day,
my right foot down pulls me forward—
the lights come brighter, haloed, red,

so I fall back, leaving distance,
cats' eyes, broken lines between us, focus
on whiteness, rime-frosted kerb and grass,

no sight now of your lights in freezing air.
And I tell myself to tell you later,
I've never known grey so beautiful,

half-light so open, winter so raw
and tender. I've never followed lights
through fog like this before.

## Breaking eggs

We choose them with exquisite care. This one
brown and long and pointed in your palm,

cold when it rolls into mine, singular as the day,
we keep till later. The second

balances across your knuckles, four fingers stretched
to stop it there. I break it, spill its eye

intact into the bowl. Two more
rest in the hollows of your collarbone,

you walk them to me   *slow  quick  slow*
then stand quite still, open the O of your mouth

to ease the fifth egg out—wet, glistening.
At last the first, a tap and crack of shell:

the cup sings. Twin yolks.
Time to feast, give thanks.

## L'heure bleue

Late sun pools on the windowsill
like that summer, warm and long—
weeks of pleasure
more acute than I had known;

I can't go back
but standing here in rose light
has the same intensity
of something nearly done.

## At the old house

There's pear blossom drifting like ash,
a broader shadow where the yew tree's spread,
the sound of a train running through April—same sound
we used to dream to

and there's you
telling me the bathroom has a shower now
in place of the narrow enamel bath,
the one we said was long enough

to hold you, six foot four,
that morning twenty years ago—
the bath so hot I went in next, lay an hour
completely sure.

Our bath's outside,
propped beneath the eaves.
Rain from the roof
has filled it to the brim.

## Arrival

Dark rain falling on grey
and no cabs near Grand Central Station.
We stop by a neon diner to look at the map

which melts as we stand in the splash
at the corner of East 38th and Park
and kiss like the first time.

Tomorrow perhaps we'll remember
the pilot's jokes on the turbulent flight,
that mad bus driver

cursing the freeway from JFK,
but for now, for once
no-one else exists, no other place,

just you and me in Manhattan,
our hearts in shock. The dark rain
flooding the street.

## Run

Manhattan's skyline panning out,
I stride west on East 58th
over Madison and Fifth, into the Park.

May: Yoshino and Kwanzan cherry blossom time,
children play in drifts. I stop to read the trees—
turkey oak and black locust, American linden,
blue atlas cedar and London plane. I chant them
jogging past the Met, north to the reservoir.

Spring, New York. Leaving winter behind,
and someone's overtaking, cutting in—
a nun on rollerblades,
black habit dancing with the breeze.

## Sum

Travel north and east until
the green sea calls you to its raggy edge

and where the spray falls
stop, fold up your fraying map.

Walk the jetty out and back
across the brine, and when you find

a bench whose seat is carved with names
turn left and left again.

If you reach the place and if it's white,
climb the steep grey stair—

put your thumb
into the stone bird's mouth.

In the fourth room there is a table
wider than the sky; sit down

and count. Don't count yourself
before the day has come.

## Recall

(i)
he finds me
as morning finds light
he is
        appetite—
my breast
the answer
        to his first question

(ii)
Kitchen nights, cocooned
in winter's black, our three-month secret
love affair, those hours by the roaring stove—

first he favoured this side, then that,
determined to fix my eyes with his,
inventing focus.

He stroked my breast as the milk came,
clamped the nipple hard between his gums
until I cried out.

My tears, then his—in turn
we shifted and swung
from pleasure to pain, and back.

## Drive time

*for Freddie*

Side by side through green sub-tropics, temperate drizzle,
thunder, early dark—twenty-five thousand miles—
we knew where we were heading. We tried
to take the right kit (thermal vests and wellingtons
are an embarrassment crossing the Nullarbor Plain).
Sunny days we wore hats, not in snow—you
loved to lower the window, thrust your bare head out,
feel crystals prickle your ears and nose. We stalled
near the South Pole. Shivering in grey Terylene
you crunched over ridges of ice to plant a flag.
That June we bumped through Amazon rainforest,
paintbox parrakeets feathering the windscreen, anacondas
sliding beneath the bumpers when we stopped
to put Brazilian air in our tyres. One blue-gold autumn
we told knock-knock jokes across the Sahara. We wintered
along the Nile playing hide-and-seek with pyramids and stars.
And when we forgot compass, calculator, maps,
your sense of direction kept us on track. From Moscow to Paris
you counted four hundred and sixty-two onion domes,
eleven hundred smoking chimney-stacks. In Tibet you said,
*Let's stay. I like temples, turmeric, himalayas*. But we drove on,
that's what we did. There's time to go round again
but you tell me your passport photo is out of date,
you're nine now, not six, or seven, or eight.

## To Freddie, my son

I wish I could take you to Assisi
a night in June. I want to take you
to the place that took us in
dream-tired, all the way from the flat north,
no hope of finding a room.

Seventeen, hair long enough to toss,
but afraid by nightfall in a dusty square—
moths mobbing the streetlamp,
the last *panini* gone.
We'd sung all the songs we knew.

She came from stone,
led us through convent doorways to a cell:
two beds, black crucifix hung between.
Below the window's splintered sill
a chipped enamel washbowl,

a pitcher of cool water
bearing the sun's dark scent. We slept
in silent absolution, woke to gauze light
over blood-tiled roofs beyond the casement,
the shock of doves on red.

## question

something's out there<br>
  listened for  not heard<br>
something like song<br>
  plucked from a bird

the bird in mind<br>
  is looked for  not seen<br>
an astonishing idea<br>
  among the green

the green's not there<br>
  but named in the head<br>
something growing<br>
  unsayable  unsaid

some things  some notes<br>
  are never found<br>
how  without these<br>
  should the music sound